EARTH'S
NATURAL
BIOMES

GRASSLAND
BIOMES

Louise and Richard Spilsbury

Crabtree Publishing Company
www.crabtreebooks.com

Crabtree Publishing Company

www.crabtreebooks.com
1-800-387-7650

Published in Canada
Crabtree Publishing
616 Welland Avenue
St. Catharines, ON
L2M 5V6

Published in the United States
Crabtree Publishing
PMB 59051
350 Fifth Ave, 59th Floor
New York, NY 10118

Published in 2018 by CRABTREE PUBLISHING COMPANY.

First published in 2017 by Wayland
Copyright © Wayland, 2017

Authors: Louise Spilsbury, Richard Spilsbury

Editors: Hayley Fairhead, Philip Gebhardt

Design: Smart Design Studio

Map (page 9) by Stefan Chabluk

Editorial director: Kathy Middleton

Proofreader: Lorna Notsch

Prepress technician: Tammy McGarr

Print and production coordinator: Margaret Amy Salter

Photographs

All photographs except where mentioned supplied by Nature Picture Library www.naturepl.com

p4, title page and back cover(r) Gerrit Vyn; p5 and imprint page(t) Denis-Huot; p6 Jeff Vanuga; p7 and imprint page(b) Denis-Huot, p8 and title page(l) De Cuveland / ARCO; p9 and back cover(l) Wild Wonder of Europe / Lesniewski; p10 (main) Neil Lucas; p11 and p31(t) David Welling; p12 and title page(t) Paul Johnson; p13 Ben Hall; p14 Pete Oxford; p15 Luiz Claudio Marigo; p16 Wim van den Heever; p17 Klein & Hubert; p18 and p30 Ingo Arndt; p19 Rolf Nussbaumer; p20 and front cover(tl) Kim Taylor; p21 Denis-Huot; p22 Laurent Geslin; p23 and front cover (tr) Anup Shah; p24 and front cover(br) Jamie Robertson; p25 Constantinos Petrinos; p26, contents page(t) and cover main Anup Shah; p27 Denis-Huot; p28 Shattil & Rozinski; p29, contents page(b) and p31(bl) Kristel Richard.

Photographs supplied by Shutterstock: p10 (inset) Chase Clausen; p12 (inset) HGalina.

Every attempt has been made to clear copyright. Should there be any inadvertent omission, please apply to the publisher for rectification.

The website addresses (URLs) included in this book were valid at the time of going to press. However, it is possible that contents or addresses may have changed since the publication of this book. No responsibility for any such changes can be accepted by either the author or the Publisher.

Printed in the USA/122019/BG20171102

Library and Archives Canada Cataloguing in Publication

Spilsbury, Louise, author
    Grassland biomes / Louise Spilsbury, Richard Spilsbury.

(Earth's natural biomes)
Includes index.
Issued in print and electronic formats.
ISBN 978-0-7787-3995-1 (hardcover).--
ISBN 978-0-7787-4123-7 (softcover).--
ISBN 978-1-4271-2005-2 (HTML)

    1. Grassland ecology--Juvenile literature. 2. Grasslands--Juvenile literature. I. Spilsbury, Richard, 1963-, author II. Title.

QH541.5.P7S66 2018   j577.4   C2017-906893-8
                                                        C2017-906894-6

Library of Congress Cataloging-in Publication Data

Names: Spilsbury, Louise, author. | Spilsbury, Richard, 1963- author.
Title: Grassland biomes / Louise Spilsbury, Richard Spilsbury.
Description: New York, New York : Crabtree Publishing Company, 2018. | Series: Earth's natural biomes | Includes index. |
Identifiers: LCCN 2017051157 (print) | LCCN 2017053955 (ebook) | ISBN 9781427120052 (Electronic HTML) | ISBN 9780778739951 (reinforced library binding) | ISBN 9780778741237 (pbk.)
Subjects: LCSH: Grassland ecology--Juvenile literature. | Grasslands--Juvenile literature. | Grassland conservation--Juvenile literature.
Classification: LCC QH541.5.P7 (ebook) | LCC QH541.5.P7 S6685 2018 (print) | DDC 577.4--dc23
LC record available at https://lccn.loc.gov/2017051157

CONTENTS

WHAT ARE GRASSLANDS?

Grasslands are wide, open areas of land that are mainly covered in grasses. As the wind blows through them, some grasslands look like giant seas of grass.

Seas of grass

Grasslands are found in places where there is just enough rain for grasses to grow, but too little rain for many trees to survive. As well as grasses, grasslands are also home to flowering plants, such as clovers and sunflowers, and shrubs, such as yuccas.

Grasses all have thread-like **roots** and long, thin leaves, but there are many different kinds of grasses in grasslands. For example, big bluestem grass can grow to 10 feet (3 m) tall. It has blue-green stems with purple or green seed heads on top. Ryegrass is a short, tufted green grass, and wild oats are medium-height grasses with dull brown stems and seed heads.

This is a grassland in Kansas, USA, with the spiky leaves and tall stems of a yucca shrub in the foreground.

Amazing Adaptation

Adaptations are special features or body parts that living things develop over time to help them survive in a biome. Grass plants have roots that spread deep and wide below the surface to collect enough water to survive dry spells.

Buzzing with life

Grasslands may look like huge, dull fields of grass, but they are buzzing with life. Millions of worms, ants, beetles, and other animals live among the grass roots underground. Insects eat grasses and seeds above ground. Birds eat seeds and make nests from dry grass. Birds, **reptiles** and other animals eat plants, insects, and each other.

Greedy grazers

The vast areas of grass also provide food for large animals, like zebras. **Grazing** animals like these spend up to 18 hours a day eating to get enough **nutrients** from grass. They are often seen together in large herds, or groups. While some animals in the herd are feeding, others can keep a lookout for **predators**, such as lions.

Lions may sneak up on a herd slowly before starting a chase across this grassland in Kenya.

Fact Focus: Biome or Habitat?

Biomes are regions of the world, such as deserts, forests, rivers, oceans, tundra, and grassland, that have a similar **climate**, plants, and animals.
A habitat is the specific place in a biome where a plant or animal lives.

DIFFERENT GRASSLANDS

There are many different grasslands around the world, but they can be split into two main kinds: temperate and tropical.

Temperate grasslands

Temperate grasslands are found in places that have warm summers, cold winters, and very little rain all year round. These biomes may have scattered trees, but there are not enough to slow down or block the wind, so they can get very blustery.

Grasses stop growing to survive the cold winters in temperate grasslands. They store water and food in their roots and save energy until the warm, damp spring comes. In spring and summer, they grow new stems, leaves, and flowers, and the sound of swishing grasses fills the air.

This temperate grassland in Wyoming, USA, gets covered in snow in winter. Bison can clear away snow with their massive heads to find grass to eat underneath.

Fact File: Hortobágy National Park

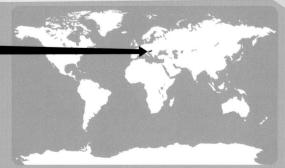

Location: Puszta, Hungary
Size: 315 sq. mi. (820 km²)
Overview: The largest temperate grassland in Europe, home to butterflies, hamsters, polecats, and saker falcons.

6

Tropical grasslands

Tropical grasslands are found in parts of the world that have two seasons: rainy and dry. Very heavy rains fall in the rainy season, which is why tropical grasslands tend to have longer grasses and scattered bushes and trees. Rains form **watering holes** that animals can drink from. During dry seasons, there is little or no rain. Most plants turn brown and stop growing. They rest until the rainy season returns. Then the plants and flowers grow rapidly again.

Tropical grassland trees have defenses to stop animals from eating them. For example, acacia trees have big, sharp thorns. But a giraffe can squeeze its extra-long tongue between the thorns and curl it around leaves to pluck them off.

Amazing Adaptation

Grasses keep on growing even after being nibbled down by hungry animals. This occurs because grasses grow from their base, near the ground, rather than from their tips as trees do.

A giraffe's long legs and neck help it to reach tasty leaves at the top of tropical grassland trees.

WHERE ARE THEY?

There are either temperate or tropical grasslands on every **continent** of the world, except Antarctica. In fact, about one quarter of Earth's land is covered with grasslands.

Tall, fluffy pampas grasses give their name to pampas grassland.

Temperate grasslands around the world

Temperate grasslands have different names in different places. The wide, flat grasslands of North America are known as prairies. Prairies have taller grasses in wetter areas and shorter plants in drier regions. Steppe grasslands are the biggest in the world. They stretch from eastern Europe to central Asia. Steppes are colder and drier than the prairies, so plants other than grasses are scarcer here. Pampas are very flat grassland between the Atlantic Ocean and the Andes mountains in South America.

Fire!

One feature that is common to grasslands all over the world is fire. In hot summers and dry seasons, wildfires spread quickly in old, dead grasses that are very dry and catch alight easily. Fires actually help grasslands because grasses grow back soon after a fire, as long as their underground roots survive. However, most trees and other plants are killed. This is another reason there are so few trees in grasslands.

This falcon is hunting animals running from the flames as a grassland fire burns.

Amazing Adaptation

In Australia, the woody seed cases of some banksia trees only open in a fire. The seeds have lots of space to grow after a fire, and ash from the fire acts like a fertilizer.

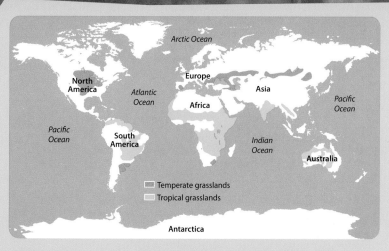

This map shows where the temperate and tropical grasslands of the world are. Grasslands are often found between areas of desert and forest.

PRAIRIE LIFE

Prairie plants and animals have different strategies for surviving the challenges of fierce wind, heat, and lack of water in the prairie grassland.

Prairie wildflowers provide nectar and seeds for insects, birds and butterflies, like this monarch butterfly.

Prairie plants

Some plants, such as ironweed, have short, tough stems to help them cope with strong winds. Many grass stems are thin and can bend in the wind, springing back up after it has passed. Indian grass and other plants grow roots up to 15 feet (4.5 m) deep to get enough water.

Amazing Adaptation

Prairie rattlesnakes are colored green and brown for **camouflage**, so they can sneak up on unsuspecting **prey** on the grassland.

Prairie animals

Crickets, wild turkeys, wolves, and many other animals live on the prairie. Prairie dogs are small, chubby animals that live in large groups. They work together to dig out huge burrows using sharp claws. They escape predators and harsh weather by hiding in tunnels underground.

Prairie dogs bite off tall plants above their burrows, so they can spot predators sneaking up on them. If one prairie dog spots danger, it cries out and the others race underground to take cover.

The heaps of mud left by the prairie dogs' digging make useful lookout posts. Prairie dogs were named because their warning cry sounds like a bark, but they are really a kind of squirrel.

A deadly bite

Prairie dogs can dive underground to escape eagles and wolves, but long, thin prairie rattlesnakes can slither after them into their burrows. The rattlesnake has two long, hollow teeth called fangs. These deadly weapons can inject **venom** into prey to kill it. Prairie rattlesnakes often live in prairie dog burrows in winter when it gets very cold. If this happens, the prairie dogs have to dig new burrows!

STEPPE LIFE

It's dry in the steppe grasslands, and although warm in the daytime and in summer, it gets very cold at night and in winter. The saiga antelope and the fierce steppe eagle are both perfectly adapted to life in this dry, chilly biome.

The saiga's eyes are at the end of bony knobs on either side of its head. They help it spot wolves and other predators coming from the side as well as from behind.

Nosing about

The saiga's nose is so long it hangs down over its mouth. This special snout has bones, hairs and **mucus** inside that help to **filter** out dust in the dry summers. It also warms up the cold air a saiga breathes in during snowy winters to stop the animal from getting too cold.

Like many other grassland grazers, saigas have long legs and hard **hooves** on their feet. Hooves help grazing animals run fast on hard ground to escape danger. Saigas can run up to 80 mph (130 km/h).

Fact Focus: Steppe Plants

Most grasses in the steppe grow less than 20 inches (50 cm) tall. The tough, thorny brambles and other shrubs living here are also short, to keep out of the path of icy winds.

Eagle-eyed predator

The steppe eagle, like many grassland birds around the world, mainly hunts from the sky. It soars over open land, watching for prey, before diving down at speeds of up to 185 mph (300 km/h). It grabs and kills small animals, such as wild hamsters, in its powerful **talons**. Then it rips its prey apart with its strong hooked beak, or swallows them whole if they are small enough.

Steppe eagles can be lazy too! They sometimes wait by burrow entrances to catch animals when they come out.

The steppe eagle has excellent eyesight. Its eyes are so big that they take up most of the space in its skull.

Fact File: The Kazakh Steppe

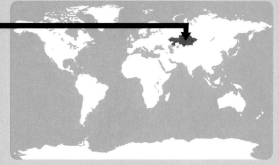

Location: It covers about 60 percent of the country of Kazakhstan.
Size: 310,500 sq. miles (804,500 km²)
Overview: One of the largest steppe regions, home to saiga antelope and wild horses.

PAMPAS LIFE

In the pampas grasslands, it's warm and windy with dry summers. There are few trees, but some areas of pampas are moister than many grasslands, so there are very tall grasses. The flat lands of the pampas are also home to some unique animals.

A sticky situation

Termites are ant-like insects that use chewed-up mud and saliva to build huge mounds. These mounds set hard like rock when they dry. The giant anteater uses its strong front legs and claws to break holes in these termite homes. Then it pokes its long, narrow snout into the holes.

Inside its long snout, the anteater has a tongue that is 20 inches (50 cm) long. It is also very sticky! The anteater shoots its tongue in and out very quickly, catching termites before they can get away and gobbling them up.

Giant anteaters can eat up to 30,000 ants and termites every day. Their long hair protects them from angry termite bites.

Fact Focus: Pampas Plants

Pampas grass (see page 8) grows in large, thick clumps. This shades the ground around the grass and stops other plants growing close to them and stealing their water.

Expert hunter

The maned wolf hunts for small animals at night or in the dim light at dusk and dawn. Its long, thin legs help it to see over the tall pampas grasses, and its huge ears help it to hear faint sounds. It can twist and turn its ears to work out exactly where an animal, like a rabbit or guinea pig, is hiding underground.

When a maned wolf hears prey in a burrow, it taps the ground with one of its front paws. This scares the animal so it runs out, and then the waiting maned wolf pounces!

Amazing Adaptation

Many pampas animals burrow into the ground to escape the heat and predators such as the maned wolf. One owl even builds its nest in underground burrows.

The maned wolf gets its name from the thick, dark mane of hair on the back of its neck that stands up when it senses danger.

SAVANNA LIFE

The savanna grassland has scattered trees and a variety of grasses, from the deep-rooted Bermuda grass to elephant grass, which can grow to 10 feet (3 m) tall. Many large animals live and feed on savanna plants.

Trunk tricks

An elephant spends about 16 hours a day eating grass, leaves, twigs, and bark. Its long, flexible trunk can wrap around a branch and snap it off or even push over a tree. The trunk also has two pointed parts at the end that work like fingers. They can grasp and remove a single leaf and pop it into the elephant's hungry mouth.

Elephants also use their trunks to suck up dust from grassland soils and spray it over themselves. This helps to prevent sunburn and blocks heat from the sun.

A layer of dust reduces the number of insect bites and stings an elephant receives on the savanna.

Big bird

Ostriches walk slowly around the grassland, eating grasses and other plants and sometimes insects. Ostriches peck at and swallow sand and small stones. These help to grind up the plant material in their stomach. An ostrich can lift up its long neck to hold its head high to search out predators. Their heads may be small, but their eyes are as big as tennis balls, so they can see to the front and sides.

The ostrich has wings, but it cannot fly. Instead, it has very long legs that it uses to run quickly away from danger. Ostriches can run twice as fast as humans!

Ostriches use their strong, long legs to run from lions, wild dogs, and hyenas, or to kick them away.

Fact File: Serengeti

Location: Tanzania and Kenya
Size: 5,700 sq. mi. (14,750 km²)
Overview: Animals that live here include lions, hyenas, cheetahs, giraffes, rhinos, zebras, and warthogs, as well as many birds, insects, and reptiles.

17

BORN SURVIVORS

Grassland animals have some amazing ways to make sure their young stay safe and survive in the biome.

Safety first

When a baby kangaroo, or a joey, is born, it's only about the size of a peanut. It crawls into its mother's comfy pouch, where it drinks milk and grows quickly. The joey stays in the pouch for at least four months. It's safe from predators in the Australian grasslands, as its mother can hop quickly away from danger. Even after the joey leaves the pouch, it still dives back in for safety or when it is tired until it's about a year old.

Amazing Adaptation

A kangaroo mother has muscles in her pouch, so she can make it go floppy to tip the joey out! She can tighten the pouch to hold on to the joey when in danger.

If a kangaroo senses danger, she can hop away at up to 25 mph (48 km/h) with her baby safely tucked inside her pouch.

A smelly start

Dung beetles are found in grasslands all over the world. The babies are called **larvae** and they have a very unusual and slightly smelly start to life! Dung beetle parents collect dung and roll it into balls that can be as big as an apple. They then work hard to push the dung balls into an underground burrow. The female lays an egg inside each dung ball. The larvae that hatch out of the eggs have an instant meal, because they eat their way out of the dung balls. The adult beetles also feed on dung.

Dung beetles have spikes on their legs to grip dung balls and roll them along.

Fact Focus: Waste Disposal Experts

Dung beetles help grasslands. Burying balls of dung helps to **recycle** nutrients back into the soil and stops grasslands from being covered in dung left by many grazing animals.

EAT OR BE EATEN

The lives of all grassland plants and animals are linked together in different food chains. **Food chains** tell the story of who eats whom in a grassland biome.

The first link in the chain

Grasses are the first link in a food chain because they make their own food. They trap the sun's energy in their leaves and use it to combine water with carbon dioxide, a gas in the air. This makes food in the form of sugars. The process is called **photosynthesis**. Plants use some of the food to grow, and they store the remainder to use later.

A food chain needs every link in order to exist. Grass needs sunlight to grow. Rabbits need grass to survive. If there are lots of rabbits, foxes have plenty to eat.

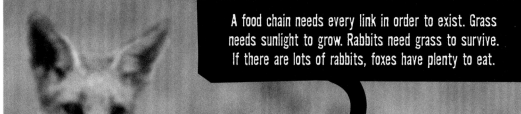

Fact Focus: Food Webs

The way several food chains connect together form **food webs**. For example, on a prairie, a mouse eats grasses and grasshoppers. Mice and grasshoppers get eaten by coyotes, owls, and snakes. Owls and coyotes eat snakes.

Hungry predators

Other grassland animals feed on the plant-eating animals to get the energy they need to survive. Lizards and snakes eat insects and **rodents**. Cheetahs catch gazelles, and lions and hyenas work in teams to bring down large grazers, such as zebras. Eagles and other birds of prey swoop from the sky to snatch small grazers while they are eating.

Amazing Adaptation

A cheetah's long legs help it run fast, and its long tail helps it steer and change direction. Both adaptations help it catch fast-moving prey on the grassland!

In one food chain, a gazelle eats grass and a cheetah eats the gazelle.

Full circle

After an animal dies, worms and tiny **bacteria** in the soil help to break down dead animal bodies and waste. When these living things **digest** and break down other animal bodies, they return nutrients to the soil. These nutrients help plants to grow and maintain food chains.

ANIMALS ON THE MOVE

Many grassland animals **migrate** long distances to find food. Saiga antelope travel 600 miles (1,000 km) north to wetter parts of the steppe for summer and return south in autumn. The sight of two million wildebeest, gazelle, and zebra migrating across the Serengeti is one of nature's greatest wonders.

Lines of migrating wildebeest can be 25 miles (40 km) long.

A dangerous journey

Rain falls at different times of the year in various parts of the Serengeti savanna. This means that herds of grazing animals migrate up to 1,850 miles (3,000 km) to follow the rains and find enough grass to survive. It is a dangerous journey. Lions chase the herds, and at river crossings there is the risk of crocodile attacks. Zebras and wildebeest often travel and feed near each other for safety. Zebras have good eyesight and wildebeest have great hearing.

Born to run

Many wildebeest and zebras have their young while travelling on migration routes. During the rainy season, there is more grass for the young animals to eat. Wildebeest calves can stand and run within minutes of being born.

Zebra foals are born feet first. Their legs are almost as long as an adult zebra's, and they can walk and even run within an hour. The young animals need to be able to keep up with the herd, or they could end up as a hungry predator's lunch.

Each zebra has a unique set of stripes, and a zebra foal learns to recognize its mother's stripe pattern, so it can easily follow her in the migrating herd.

Amazing Adaptation

Some scientists think that the stripes of all the zebras in a herd blend together to confuse lions so that they have trouble picking out one zebra to chase and attack.

GRASSLAND PEOPLE

More people live on grasslands than on any other biome in the world. Grasslands also feed more people than any other biome.

Fields of grass

Grassland soils are ideal for growing **crops** or raising **livestock**. Instead of wild grasses, many areas of grassland have been replanted by people with other grass-like plants that they and their animals can eat, such as barley, wheat, rice, and other grains. There are also vast areas of grassland where farmers and ranchers raise huge herds of farm animals, such as sheep and cattle.

Amazing Adaptation

Grasslands have healthy soils because when their many underground roots die, bacteria and other **decomposers** release nutrients from them. This helps other plants to grow.

Ranchers round up huge herds of their cattle that roam across enormous areas of land in the grasslands of Queensland, Australia.

Home on the biome

As the world's population increases, people are spreading farther and farther into grasslands. Grasslands are often on flat areas of land that are easy to build on. Grasses are easier to remove than thick forests, and many of these biomes also have a climate people can live in. By building their houses, offices, factories, or even parks and golf courses on grasslands, people destroy grassland habitats.

On safari

People also enjoy visiting grassland biomes, such as the savanna, to see the wildlife. This gives tourists a better understanding of grasslands and their animals and makes it more likely that they will help to protect them. The money tourists pay helps people protect areas of savanna. However, tourist jeeps can damage grasslands, and crowds of people can disturb animals and interrupt their feeding or **breeding**.

Safari vehicles crowd into an area near the Mara River, so tourists can see wildebeest and zebra during the Serengeti migration season.

Fact Focus: Disappearing Prairies

Only about one percent of the North American wild prairie grasslands still exists. Most have been taken over by people for farms or towns.

GRASSLAND THREATS

Grassland biomes look like tough, wild places, but in fact they are fragile because water is so scarce. When grasslands are in danger, the wildlife in them is too.

Drying up

Cities and farms use large amounts of water. Farmers may also use strong chemicals to kill weeds that kill wild plants. Their huge numbers of goats and cows eat the grasses and pull them up by their roots. Without water and without plants to hold the soil together, the nutrient-rich **topsoil** dries up and blows away, and the land becomes dusty and bare.

Another problem is that **global warming** is causing temperatures around the world to increase. As parts of the world get hotter, the amount of rain that falls and when it falls also changes. Grasslands are already short of water, so this increases the risk that grasslands will dry up completely.

If watering holes dry up, grassland animals like these thirsty lions may not be able to get enough water to survive.

Animals under threat

When grasslands lose their plant life, or people take over grasslands for farms or towns, animals have nothing to eat and nowhere to live. Animal food chains get broken. If there is not enough grass to support large numbers of grazing animals like zebras, there will not be enough food for animals, such as lions, that eat the grazers.

Animals face other dangers, too. Some are treated as pests to stop them from eating crops. Farmers have killed about 98 percent of all prairie dogs to stop horses and cows from being hurt by falling into prairie dog holes. On the savanna, people catch and kill animals, such as cheetahs and rhinos, for their fur or horns.

People kill rhinos for their horns, which are then crushed and used to make traditional medicines.

Fact Focus: Endangered Animals

Human actions in grasslands have left many animals in danger of extinction, or dying out forever. Endangered grassland animals include cheetahs, African wild dogs, black rhinos, and many more.

GRASSLAND FUTURES

Grasslands are very special biomes that are home to some of the world's most amazing animals, so people are working hard to protect them for the future.

Scientists gently attach bands to burrowing owls to track their movement through a grassland.

Expert advice

Scientists study grasslands and their wildlife to understand what they need to survive and how to help them. For example, grasslands need some fires to stop too many trees from growing, so scientists advise people who manage grasslands to allow controlled fires to burn rather than put them out.

Caring for the land

People are also learning how to care for the soil and grasses. They protect and restore areas of water, which grasslands need to survive. They plant trees around the edges of grasslands to act as windbreaks to stop the topsoil blowing away. Farmers help by allowing parcels of land to recover before letting livestock graze on it again.

National parks

Governments turn some areas of grassland into **national parks**. This protects them by law. People can visit to enjoy the wildlife and scenery, but they cannot disturb or harm the animals or their habitat. No hunting is allowed, and there is a limit on the number of roads that can be built and the amount of water people can use.

Taking action

You can help to protect grasslands too. You could adopt an endangered grassland animal. The money you pay helps people protect those animals. Or you could write to government officials to ask what they are doing to help protect the world's grasslands or the grasslands in your country. You could learn more about grasslands and their wildlife and tell other people about how important these biomes are.

Wild Przewalski's horses were bred in zoos and then returned to their natural habitat to avoid extinction.

Fact Focus: The Last Wild Horses

Przewalski's horses are the last of the world's truly wild horses. They were in danger of becoming **extinct**, until they were brought back to Hustai National Park in Mongolia.

GLOSSARY

adaptation Special feature or way of behaving that helps a living thing survive in its habitat

bacteria Tiny living things that can cause diseases or decompose waste

biome Large region of Earth with living things adapted to the typical climate, soils, and other features.

breeding Having young

camouflage Color, pattern, or shape that makes it hard to identify an object against the background it is in

climate Typical weather pattern through the year in an area

continent One of the seven large masses of land on the planet: Asia, Africa, North America, South America, Europe, Australia and Antarctica

crop Plant grown for food

decomposers Living things, such as bacteria and fungi, that break down bits of dead plants and animals and waste into nutrients plants can use to grow

digest Break down food into nutrients, usually inside the stomach and intestines

extinct When every individual plant or animal of a particular kind has died out

filter Pass something through something with tiny holes to remove unwanted material

food chain A way of showing the movement of the sun's energy from one living thing to another

food web A network of related food chains that shows how energy is passed from one living thing to another

global warming Rise in average temperature of Earth caused by human use of machines and electricity that is altering weather patterns worldwide

grazing Feeding on grass

habitat Place where an animal or plant typically lives

hoof Hard covering over animal toes

larvae Stage in development that some animals go through before becoming adults

livestock Farm animals

migrate Move from one place to another, normally in search of something

mucus Slimy substance produced by the body for lubrication and protection

national park An area in nature where the wildlife is protected by law

nutrients Substances living things need to live and grow

photosynthesis Process by which green plants make sugary food using the energy in sunlight

predator Animal that catches and eats other animals

prey Animal eaten by another animal

recycle To make something new from something used before

reptile A snake, lizard, or other animal that is cold-blooded, lays eggs, and has a body covered with scales or bony plates

rodent Animal with large front teeth for gnawing, such as a mouse

roots Underground parts of a plant that take in water and nutrients from the soil

talons Bird claws

topsoil Top layer of soil that contains the nutrients plants need to grow

venom Poison made by some animals for defense or to stun or kill prey

watering hole Pool of water from which animals regularly drink

FIND OUT MORE

Books
Grasslands Inside Out (Ecosystems Inside Out)
James Bow
Crabtree Publishing Company, 2015

Grassland Food Webs in Action
(Searchlight Books: What Is a Food Web?)
Paul Fleisher
Lerner Classroom, 2015

Serengeti Research Journal (Ecosystems Research Journal)
Natalie Hyde
Crabtree Publishing Company, 2018

WEBSITES AND WEBCAMS

You can see videos, facts, and images about grasslands at:

**www.bbc.co.uk/nature/habitats/temperate_grasslands,_savannas,_
and_shrublands**

Watch the animals that visit a watering hole in grasslands at:

explore.org/live-cams/player/african-watering-hole-animal-camera

Find out more about threats grasslands face and what is being done
to protect them at:

www.worldwildlife.org/habitats/grasslands

There is more information about savannas at:

www.cotf.edu/ete/modules/msese/earthsysflr/savannah.html

INDEX